P•E•A•K

PEAK METHOD

A practical and proven approach to actualizing your best life by managing the hours in your day

SUSAN FLEMING

THE RELAXATION CENTER

BELMONT, CALIFORNIA

Published by
The Relaxation Center
Belmont, California, USA

First printed in 2013.

ISBN: 978-0-9849084-0-0

Copyright © 2011 by Susan Fleming, The Relaxation Center

All rights reserved. No part of this book may be used or reproduced in any manner whatsoever without the prior written permission of the Publisher.

Printed in the United States of America.
For information, contact The Relaxation Center
<www.therelaxationcenter.com>

Photography by BruceFlemingPhotography.com

Book Design by Ann Miller – M2 Design: www.pennib.com
Text set in Minion Pro.

Library of Congress Cataloging-in-Publication Data

Fleming, Susan

PEAK Method / Susan Fleming

TXu 1-783-515

Self Improvement

DEDICATION

*This book is dedicated to Ann Miller
for helping me put my life experiences
on paper so that others may
benefit from my findings and accomplish their own
physical, spiritual and mental well-being.*

TABLE OF CONTENTS

Foreword i

What is the PEAK Method? ii

Introduction iii

My Story iv

How To Use This Book 1

PART ONE: PEAK Method Study Guide 2

The PEAK Method Process 3

The Basics of Practicing PEAK 9

The Color Blue 10

The PEAK Method Mantra 11

PART TWO: PEAK Method Workbook 13

LESSON 1: Your Life Today 14

LESSON 2: Digging into Today and Creating Tomorrow 19

LESSON 3: Designing your PEAK Life 22

LESSON 4: Making your PEAK Life a Reality 28

PEAK Method Review 29

About the Author 31

My Notes 32

Extra PEAK Method Worksheets 33

Foreword

When I was 11 years old, I asked my mother what my purpose was on earth. She gave me a good answer I believe. She said there were two purposes. The first was biological, basically to reproduce if that is your choice. The second purpose was to become the best person you can. I was speechless after that answer. It gave me much to think about and I have been thinking about it to this moment. After she died, I found a motivational document among her papers and framed it. I really took it to heart. Whenever I read it, I feel compelled to get up and dust myself off and get back on the horse and get riding. I hope you take time to read this and really feel the motivation. —SUSAN FLEMING

Youth is not a time of life ... it is a state of mind.

It is not a matter of rosy cheeks, red lips and supple knees; it is a matter of the will, a quality of the imagination, a vigor of the emotions, and the freshness of the deep springs of life.

Youth means a temperamental predominance of courage over timidity, and an appetite for adventure over the love of ease. This often exists in a man of sixty more than a boy of twenty. Nobody grows old merely by living a number of years. We grow old only by deserting our ideals.

Years may wrinkle the skin, but to give up enthusiasm wrinkles the soul. Worry, fear, self-distrust and despair bow the head and turn the spirit back to dust.

Whether sixty or sixteen, there is in every human being's heart the lure of wonder, the unfailing child-like appetite for what's next, and the joy of the game of living. You are as young as your faith, as old as your doubt; as young as your self-confidence, as old as your fear; as young as your hope, as old as your despair. In the center of your heart and my heart there is a wireless station; so long as it receives messages of beauty, hope, cheer, courage, and power from the earth, from men and from the infinite, so long are you young.

When the aerials are all down and your spirit is covered with the snows of cynicism and the ice of pessimism, then you have grown old indeed.

SAMUEL ULLMAN

What is the PEAK Method?

The **PEAK Method** is a personal management system that can trigger beneficial changes in daily life experience. Using the **PEAK Method**, it is possible to change a habitual and repetitive daily life pattern toward a more flexible lifestyle that can provide satisfying results.

The **PEAK Method** is a system of customizable guides and charts that help promote clear thinking. It provides a simple framework that makes it easy to target personal goals and achieve beneficial outcomes.

Introduction

How I Developed The PEAK Method

The **PEAK Method** is a system you can use to get out of a rut or depression, to motivate you to seek a better situation, or just to improve your daily life by using your time to achieve specific goals.

The secret of PEAK is within the story of my life. Looking back on the key events in my life, I realize that I have been developing my positive attitude and the foundation for what I now call the **PEAK Method**.

This approach to life began to evolve when I was three years old because of a tragic accident. The accident and its aftermath taught me how to survive immense physical pain. The way I instinctively coped at that early age is how I have coped with all difficult times thereafter. In-depth detail follows in the next section, "My Story."

So here it is for you. The **PEAK Method** can help anyone who wants to make a positive change in their life. With the **PEAK Method** you take responsibility for what you indeed have the capability to change. You may even discover new things you want to change, as your ability to change increases.

Sometimes when things are very difficult we may feel overwhelmed or, like that old saying, that we've gone from the frying pan into the fire. The **PEAK Method** can help you not only get out of the fire but get off the stove altogether and take charge of your situation.

As you learn about the **PEAK Method**, you may become resistant, skeptical or want to close the book. The **PEAK Method** is designed to challenge you to see the truth in yourself and finally be able to achieve your goals in life. I encourage you to stick with it and see for yourself how you can utilize the **PEAK Method**. I know it will work for you as it continues to work for me.

SUSAN FLEMING

*Use the **PEAK Method** to bring you to your personal best.*

My Story

The will to live well

Please read my story now (or come back to it later) to understand the reasons for the **PEAK Method** coming together as a life action plan. I believe understanding this will help you to understand your own process of change.

Let me tell you about some pivotal events in my life that led to my distilling this method of making positive changes happen no matter what. We all have situations in our lives that just happen to us. During my very challenging times, I was convinced there was something I could do to change my current life for the better. I share these experiences with you and hope that you will use your inner power to change what you can change in order to have your best life.

The Accident

When I was three, my parents started a barbecue outside and left me out there while they went in to get some things. I had my red and white striped nightgown on and wandered over to see the little fire, which was in one of those low hibachis. I felt the warmth of the fire and lifted my nightgown up over it; the nightgown caught on fire. I started screaming and my father came out and rolled me on the grass to put the flames out. He carried me inside and my mother put me in the sink with cold water. Then they took me to the hospital. I remember hearing, "You've got to live, I love you."

I was in the hospital for months, waiting to recover. Eighty percent of my body was burned. I didn't realize until much later how guilty my parents had felt.

Physical Pain

After I healed a bit, I had to have skin grafts. They took skin from my back side and put it on my right leg to save the 3rd degree burned area, which was the whole front of my thigh. Days later they had to remove the gauze patches from the back side of my body, from where they had taken the skin. I remember as clearly as if it were today, being in a soaking tub with the horrible pain of the nurse trying to rip off the gauze. I screamed at the intense pain. She said, "We have to get these patches off, they can't stay on." Right then I learned how to push the pain away and mentally move into the future, while physically remaining in the present, bearing the pain of what needed to happen and being strong enough to know that the immediate pain—which was less intense than the initial 80% burn—would go away. I knew I could handle it. At that age, in my mind, I realized that there were stages in the healing process. I thought: "You can do it" (being positive), "Come on, it's ok" (enthusiastic), "You're getting through this experience" (action) and you have discovered the ability to change and get relief, "You did it, Susan" (new knowledge). Since that time, nothing in my life has been so physically painful, but I learned an important lesson.

Mental Pain

School was a normal process all the way through fifth grade. Then we moved to a new town after my parents got divorced. I had to walk to school in a skirt, which we had to wear at that time. I was afraid to go to school because the kids could see the burn on my leg and I knew they would ask me about it. Where I used to live, everyone already knew I had been burned. The new kids would be certain to ask me, and they did. I felt ugly and rejected. I was the different one. I thought about it as I was "the only one in this class of people." African American people had others like them, Asian people had people like them, and so on. But burned people don't have anyone else. I would not look anyone straight in the eye, so they would not have the opportunity to ask what happened to me. Some kids would say things like "give it to the girl with the burn." It was my main identity. I wished I had died in the fire at those moments; I felt like the school freak.

But I had to go to school and said to myself, "Be positive, you can do it," and I did it, regardless of the consequences, and learned I could get through it. I heard my mom say, "You'll be fine."

Years later I had a date with a guy who said "I am not going out with you again; that scar is too much for me." Wow, I was so hurt in my heart, and felt the ugliest ever. Why me with the horrible scar? That scar forced me to realize early in life how to overcome a major obstacle and live with hope and strength to have a better life, which is what the **PEAK Method** is all about.

Emotional Pain

Beyond the physical and mental anguish and emotional pain associated with the burn, there were additional stressful factors that were not necessarily burn-related. These could happen to anyone.

When I was 9 years old, my parents were sitting on the couch and announced they were getting a divorce. I felt like my heart was being ripped in two. I knew my life would never be the same.

When I was 16, I wanted more reconstructive surgery and visited my old doctor to see if he could fix the scar tissue on my leg. He couldn't believe I had lived through so much, that I was even there. He said I was a miracle child to survive that burn, but it turned out there was nothing more he could do.

When I was 18, my mother became terminally ill and asked me to take care of her. Setting aside my personal plans, I did this until she passed away two years later. I had to give up my scholarship for engineering school and then develop a new life strategy. Again I used the **PEAK Method** to pursue my personal development.

Discovering the Ability to Change

When we are little, we are vulnerable. If we are injured, we blame ourselves. We get emotionally scarred when we are not understood by adults. We grow up coming from a damaged place, feeling we are less than we should be. We see others having fun and being happy, and ask ourselves questions. "Why am I not happy?" "How can I be like others appear to be?" "Is their happiness really the truth?" "How can I become fulfilled in myself, and be joyful?"

The quest begins. We look in every corner. Will this work? Will that? We keep looking! We know the truth is under it all, and that something is not right. In my story I pursued the options.

Help from Others

Leading life with a blanket over my head and in a perpetual disabling fear of connection with others soon brought me to the inevitable obstacles that had to be overcome. I somehow had to interact in public.

I started taking speech classes and ran out of the first session, my heart pounding in fear. I took acting classes and had a nervous freakout meltdown at the first challenge. It seemed hopeless that I could ever make any change.

Slowly I realized that my fear was turning into anger, and I was determined to do something about it. I finally contacted a well known national institute for speech and self-improvement. I signed up for a class in public speaking; this went well, except that I stared down at my feet while giving my presentation. The teacher told me not to look at the huge crowd in the audience, but to pick one friendly face in the crowd and at least look up at that one face. This moment was the beginning of coming out of my shell. To that point I had not realized that I had been looking down to avoid eye contact. And at that point I realized that I could indeed make a change!

Then I went to a meeting of an international club that promotes public speaking skills. Each of us in my local group had a chance to do a very simple task. My assignment that day was to be the person in charge of current event topics. A high-ranking club member was a guest that day and I asked her if she would participate in our 2-minute discussion topic. She agreed and I then asked my question, expecting the prescribed and truthful answer. When the Grand Poobah (as I now refer to her) began to speak, to my utter surprise she said, "I choose not to talk about that topic today. Instead, I would like to talk about this..." I heard it loud and clear. I was free. I could be like her and choose my own topic in any conversation anywhere. I didn't have to answer to everyone as I had been doing, and I didn't have to exist to meet expectations any more. This was a huge breakthrough.

Power

To gain personal strength you have to get rid of what's not working. Get a new bulb, twist it in the socket, and turn on the light. Reconnect. Cleanse. Enliven your life. Take the steps to open your eyes and improve your life. Go from your worst to your best.

I can't compare my worst to anyone else's worst. I have seen many people with greater misfortune, but we live on. It is our own responsibility to improve our situation, for our own peace of mind and overall benefit, and because no one else is going to do it. Just keep going. Enjoy building your strength, solving problems, overcoming obstacles. My accident at three years of age was both a gift and a curse. Because of enduring so much I have great empathy for every living being on the planet.

Basket of Goodness

I wanted to replace that sad, shy, hunched, withdrawn person with the Susan who could be 100% present anywhere on her own agenda, loving, kind, with positive energy overflowing and a sense of strength, compassion, and oneness. With my personal determination I went from a place where it was impossible to talk and share to a place where it is natural and easy to talk and share.

During the next phase of my life I invested 15 years in the hotel and restaurant business working with people and managing teams. I came to understand that everyone—customers, employees, mothers, fathers, children, athletes, and so on—experiences stress in their lives.

In my current life as a coach, trainer, and deep tissue massage therapist, and having worked for the last 20 years with people experiencing chronic pain, I have seen many conditions in the course of each day.

These years of experience made me aware of the many causes of stress. When stress is internalized it develops into tightness in the body. It can be emotional stress, or repetitive stress, or ergonomic stress, to name a few. If not recognized and counteracted, stress can develop into a destructive force on one's health.

From an objective viewpoint, making logical changes seems manageable. The **PEAK Method** enables one to view one's life from a more objective perspective. Understanding this, one can add a positive attitude, enthusiasm, and action to lead toward a more stress-free life and to be healthier and happier every day. The sooner ones starts, the better off one will be.

Making the PEAK Method Stronger: Helping Others

One day a client arrived for her first massage. She expressed discomfort because she felt too overweight to get a massage. I explained that I was massaging her spirit and that her physical body was what we were working on at that moment. It was important to make her spirit feel great and build her confidence and reconnect to her body with a sense of vitality. She seemed to relax and enjoy the massage. She came back every month and I noticed that she had lost some weight. She said that inside she felt happy after I told her we wanted to make her spirit feel great. She had been to the grocery store and bought a book on how to quit being a carbohydrate addict; she read the book and was following it. Since then she has made other changes in her life one step at a time, all based on wanting to keep her feelings positive. That is what it is all about.

As I learned from my mother, we are fine as we are, wherever we are with our lives. It is what we do in each moment to make it better that counts. We don't have to be this or that. We just need to make our spirit better by making good choices and taking action every moment.

Putting the PEAK Method Into Words

I had been using The **PEAK Method** as a natural part of my life and one day I was sitting at home alone recuperating from foot surgery, and I felt myself reflecting on how as a 3-year-old I got through the healing period after my burn. I said the familiar four steps out loud to myself and then wrote them down for the first time. A few days later I shared these four steps with a client; he was excited to hear this and wanted to apply the method to his life. I thought it seemed so simple yet so logical, so I decided to write it down for everyone. Using this system will help you get out of a rut or depression, motivate you to seek a better situation, or improve your daily life. You can begin to live well by actively using your time to achieve your own specific goals. ***Time is your tool.***

Now it's time for you to turn the page and get started on your own journey to PEAK living. I'm here for you. Let's get started!

Time is your tool.

This time chart graphic is a reminder that you are the designer of your day. Defining your activities and timing increases your power over the results.

The PEAK Method Study Guide and Workbook will enable you to:

- Assess how your life is structured now
- Target areas of your life for improvement
- Identify and make your desired changes

PEAK METHOD

How To Use This Book

The book is divided into two parts: study guide and workbook.
Read both parts through to get a good overview.
Then start again at the beginning, reading and thinking about every word.

Part One – A study guide that explains the concept and method.

Part Two – A workbook in which you learn to apply PEAK to your life.

Let the material sink in either slowly or quickly. You will "get it"—it's not complicated—and when you use this method, it will be worth it.

YOU CAN DO IT!
Open yourself to change. It's up to you to take the first step.

There are many self-improvement programs on the market today. The **PEAK Method** is not intended to replace these programs but to enhance and improve their effectiveness. Even if you are not using another program, following the **PEAK Method** will help you shift your perspective and get ready for positive change, putting your own improvement into a priority position. The **PEAK Method** is the key to self-improvement success. It will guide you forward to your overall personal best.

PEAK METHOD

PART ONE
PEAK Method Study Guide

Understanding the PEAK Method

*Study the P.E.A.K. Method
and learn how it works*

The PEAK Method Process

Practicing the **PEAK Method** will enable you to be at your "peak" best more often. PEAK is an intellectual description of the way to change behaviors by training the subconscious mind to be in alignment with the conscious mind. It is a process of learning to be aware and making changes for a better life. The **PEAK Method** will teach you to make "feeling your best" be your default behavior. If you're not feeling your best, you can identify what is holding you back and then minimize or remove it. Finally, with practice, you can change your perspective and your mindset.

A change like this is not just for you and for me as individuals. We can positively influence others. The process of PEAK is powerful and its explanation appears simple to understand. Simple is not always easy and it takes dedication to apply, especially at first. The **PEAK Method** is designed to help you identify, incorporate, and actualize your desired life as closely as possible.

```
P = Positive
E = Enthusiastic
A = Action
K = Knowledge
```

*PEAK asks you to choose to be Positive and Enthusiastic,
to take Action and gain Knowledge as the basis for your life.*

DRINK, HORSE, DRINK
"You can lead a horse to water, but you can't make him drink."

Just like the proverbial horse, you get to make a choice for change. It's your feelings about your life that teach you that you need to drink the "water." The **PEAK Method** shows you *how* to drink the water to make a change.

POSITIVE • ENTHUSIASTIC • ACTION • KNOWLEDGE

Use the PEAK Method to Bring You to Your Best

The **PEAK Method** guides you through four main steps:

1) adopting a **positive** attitude, 2) maintaining an **enthusiastic** approach, 3) taking **action**, and 4) acquiring the **knowledge** to keep you on the path to being your best.

The **PEAK Method** is best explained as a cycle of self-reflection leading to action. This visualization shows all four stages of the process.

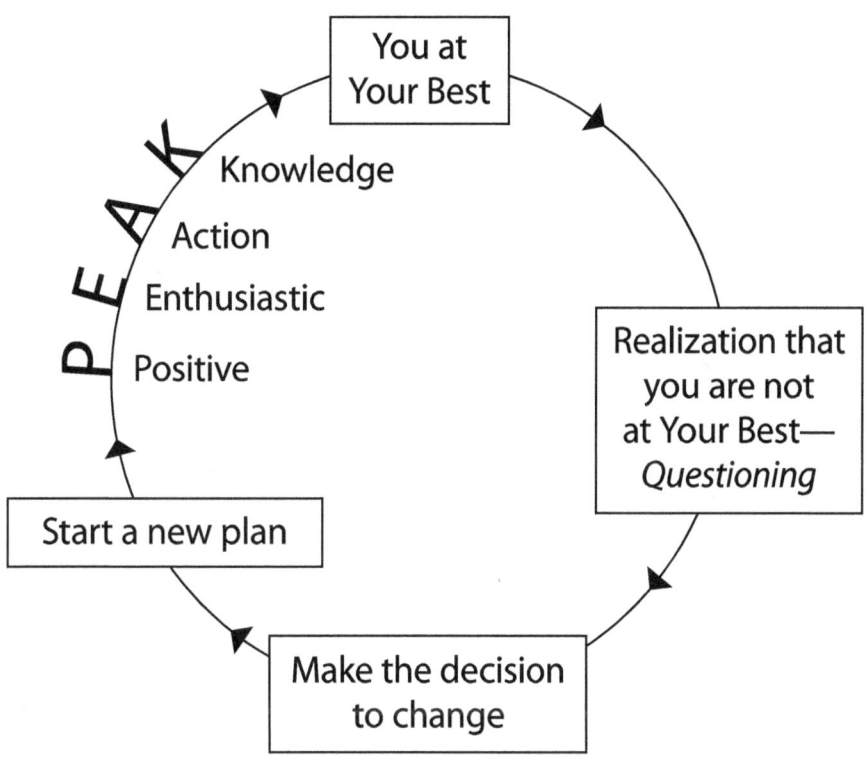

*Use the **PEAK Method** to bring you to Your Best.*

The above chart you'll see again and again. Using it is the basis for actualizing the **PEAK Method** in your life. This method is powerful because it takes your unrealized ideas and transforms them into concrete items you can see and touch. Following the **PEAK Method** leads you one step at a time to help you realize your goals. Part One of this book identifies the four stages of development for personal growth. Part Two guides you to identify obstacles while targeting personal strengths to develop and life skills to add.

ASK YOURSELF

What is my best?
Am I at my best?
How does it feel to be at my best?

You at Your Best

You at Your Best means feeling your best and being the Best You. By utilizing the **PEAK Method** you can examine all the factors in your current life. By focusing on one area at a time, you can clarify your goals. Your Best is at the top of the circle because it symbolizes being at the top of your game, your performance in life. By using the **PEAK Method** your quality of life can improve far beyond your expectations.

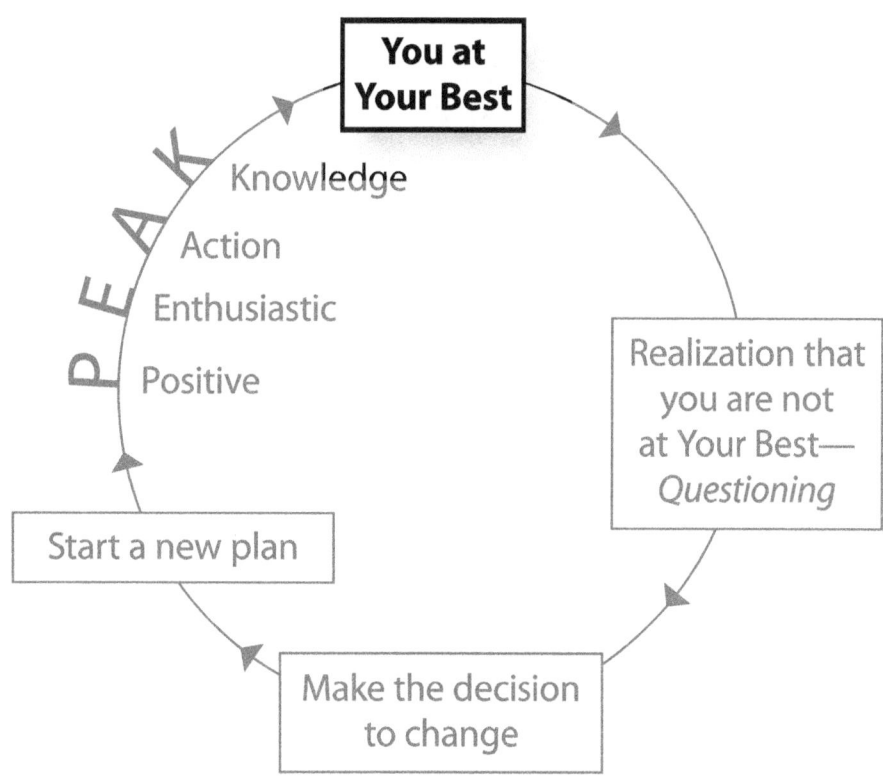

Being the Best You is a choice, made possible by intention and action. Thinking about the Best You will guide you to create a picture of what you want your life to contain. The **PEAK Method** helps you to put positive and desired steps to take on your daily calendar.

ASK YOURSELF

What is happening when I'm not at my best?
What is missing in my life?
Am I feeling negative or dissatisfied?
I'm not feeling "right"— what can I do to feel better?

> **Realization that you are not at Your Best— *Questioning***

The **realization** that you are not at your best leads to **questioning**, which leads to making the decision to change.

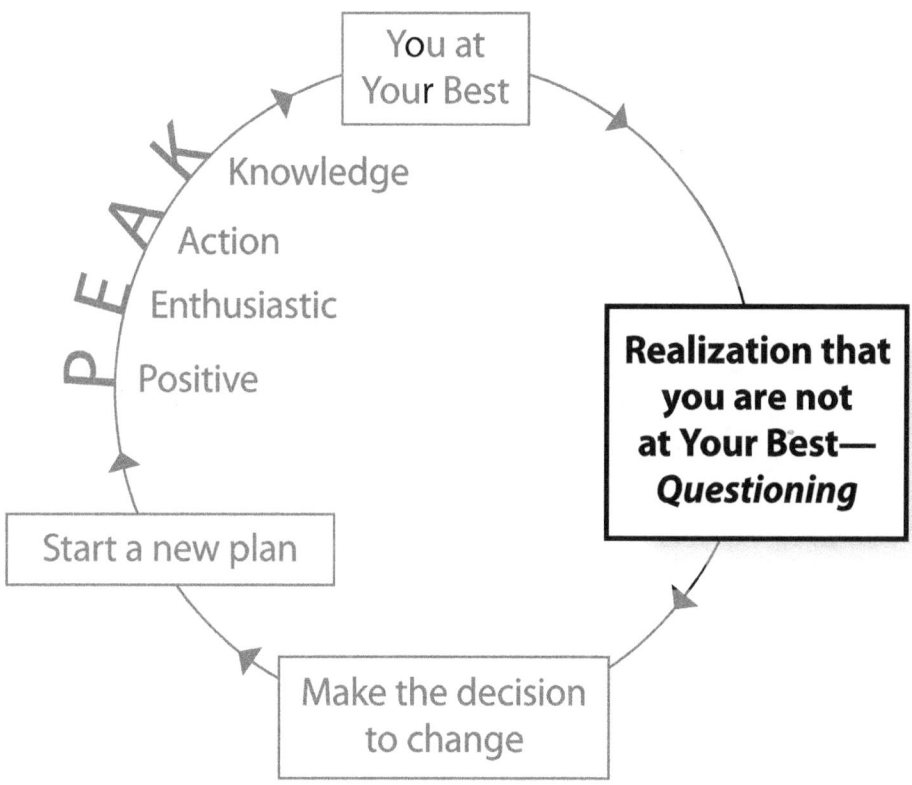

Self-assessment is a natural, ongoing process of reviewing the events and actions of your day. Personal power comes from learning to examine your daily actions under a microscope, observing the data dispassionately, like a scientist, and creating new habits based on your own research and reflection. Habits create our day, and creating new habits empowers the self to achieve new awareness. There is no need ever to be discouraged. When you focus on PEAK, this method will work naturally for you.

ASK YOURSELF

What is preventing me from being engaged
in a vibrant life experience?
What do I need to let go of to reach my best?
What can I add to my day right now
to make my life better?

> **Make the decision to change**

When you make the **decision to change**, you take charge and make a new action plan. You commit to working your way toward your best.

In a 24-hour day, in each moment, you are making choices that shape your life and the lives of those around you. It is your choice to be responsible for your own improvement.

ASK YOURSELF

What is a better plan?
How can I improve my life?

Start a new plan

To **start a new plan** means to erase, replace or minimize what's not working for you, and to focus on making a real change.

Think about typical obstacles, negatives, non-essentials and time-wasters. We can all feel overwhelmed at times and seek distractions. Overindulging in such things as TV, snack foods, video games, social media or texting can throw us off track. Blaming a situation or other people for our own lack of performance is non-productive. Hiding from action by sleeping or zoning out, whatever means you use, is another way of not reaching one's potential. Learn to identify and distinguish between beneficial escapes and harmful ones. Real relaxation is legitimate and necessary.

The Basics of Practicing PEAK

P stands for Positive

Whatever change(s) you decide to make, start by believing in your ability to make the change. Believe in your worth and in your improved future.

TELL YOURSELF "I can do this! I am able in every way to change toward my goal." Or just say the word "positive" to yourself.

Say out loud to yourself one action or one step to take toward a goal.

E stands for Enthusiastic

Enthusiasm will energize you and give you the momentum you need to have the life you want.

ASK YOURSELF What word or phrase comes to mind when you think about encouraging someone and praising a good effort? It might be a child in your care, your favorite sports team, a student, or a good friend. Brainstorm a list of what comes naturally to you. It might be something like "Go for it!" or "You can do it!" The key here is to find a word or phrase you can use to encourage yourself as enthusiastically as you would encourage another.

TELL YOURSELF "Go for it!" "You can do it!" or whatever word or phrase motivates you to feel positively energized.

Push yourself forward in the new direction.

A stands for Action

Follow your plan and take at least one step of the many steps you need to take. Keep adding steps as you progress. Your best self is waiting for you!

TELL YOURSELF "I did it!" "Great job!" Action leads to results. Eliminate non-essentials. Take even one little step that specifically relates to your main goal.

Do one sit-up. Eat one carrot.

K stands for Knowledge

A successful cycle through the **PEAK Method** brings you closer to your best self and gives you the know-how, the courage, and the power to continue making changes any time you find that you are not at your best. New knowledge changes your way of thinking.

TELL YOURSELF "I have new knowledge. Because I took this one step, I can now keep taking more steps toward my goal."

Say this every time you do a PEAK cycle, reinforcing your motivation.

The Color Blue

Once you understand the **PEAK Method** you will be compelled to improve your life. When you know *how* to change your life, it is impossible to settle for less. It is like never having seen the color blue. If someone then shows you the color blue, you will always know exactly what the color blue is. You can never unlearn knowing the color blue.

It is the same with the **PEAK Method**. Make the time to understand and apply this concept and you will watch your life begin to change. Everyone has their own speed of changing. It is up to you to do the best you can in order to have the life you deserve. You can do it.

For example, the PEAK Method can help you...

> Get out of your rut in life
> Stop being depressed
> Really lose weight, finally
> Take ownership of your day

The PEAK Method can help you improve any aspect of your life!

TELL YOURSELF
"I have acquired the knowledge and skills to change any area of my life that I wish.

Time is your tool.

You are the designer of your day. When you define your activities and timing you will increase power over results.

The PEAK Method Mantra

Use the PEAK Method Mantra by vocalizing:

Using the **PEAK Method** in different ways makes it an integrated part of your life. **Say it OUT LOUD** whenever you start to feel "not right." **This is the KEY.** Vocalizing the mantra creates vibrations in the body and makes it a physical experience, a stronger reality. You can also write the **PEAK Method** Mantra down on paper to make it more concrete.

Even if you feel uncomfortable with vocalizing, just go ahead and say it and you will learn to believe in your real self as you make steps toward being your best. Just practice. Practicing is the important part.

SAY THE PEAK MANTRA OUT LOUD

Positive (or say "I can do this")

Enthusiastic (or say "I'm going for it")

Action ("I'm taking this first specific step")

Knowledge (acknowledge your effort: "I did a good job! I made it.")
You have changed your mindset by doing these steps. [refer to p. 9 "Basics"]

Utilize the **PEAK Method** to make little changes that in time add up to big changes.

HERE ARE SOME SPECIFIC EXAMPLES:

You want to get a better job.

Positive – Say the positive words "I really want this position."

Enthusiastic – Say "This job is a great fit! I will go for it!"

Action – Ask yourself "What action can I take right now toward getting a new job? Maybe I can improve my appearance; new clothes might be a first step." *Take action by going to the store and having the clerk help you select a good looking outfit.*

Knowledge – Say "I have new knowledge. I did it. I took a step toward getting my new job. I feel better and look better. This is one of the steps to getting there. Now that I have done one step I can do another. I am going to keep taking steps until I get that job!"

You want to get more clients for your business.

Positive – Say the words out loud: "I'm positive."

Enthusiastic – Say "I have much to contribute; my clients need my help!"

Action – Ask yourself "What action can I take to get more business? I can email five prospective clients and let them know that I am now offering a half price seasonal special."

Take the single action of emailing one of the five individuals, which can be repeated daily.

Knowledge – Say "I have new knowledge of performing an action. After several days I have actually emailed five clients, taking individual steps toward getting more business. I am one step closer to being busier and more successful. I am going to keep making the effort. I am going to try new approaches. I am going to observe and learn new ways, and be willing to improve with the changes that continue to happen. I am going to be flexible and take action to transform myself and my business."

SAY THE PEAK MANTRA OUT LOUD, AGAIN AND AGAIN

Say it again and do it again and keep going again and again your whole life. It is a way of life and a great life.

The cycle of life is always a renewal. Renewal can happen each minute of each hour of each day of your whole life. As you take time to reflect and set aside time each day for personal positive action, you will be exercising the **PEAK Method**.

Congratulations on thoughtfully completing Part One!

Time is your tool.

You are the designer of your day.

PEAK METHOD

PART TWO
PEAK Method Workbook

Activating the PEAK Method

*Put your vision into action
and get real results*

LESSON 1:
Your Life Today

Use the following pages for personal assessment and development. They will help you visualize how to change. Keep a notebook and a paper or digital calendar, something you will use on a daily basis.

This first lesson is about learning to assess how your life is structured now. Worksheets 1 and 2 will help you map this out. On the following pages you will see samples of both of these worksheets followed by blank versions for you to complete.

Take your time completing both of these worksheets. You will most likely be surprised at what you see.

Trust the **PEAK Method** as your key to success!

Sample Worksheet 1
Assess how your life is structured now

ASK YOURSELF

What are the major and minor factors in your life now?
Are you happy?
Does your life feel balanced?
Is there too much work, not enough sleep or exercise?
Is there too much play, or not enough?

Divide your day (or week) into sections following the sample below. On the next page, you will see a sample schedule to help you calculate how much time you invest doing different things. Then you will create a pie chart (see page 17) similar to the one below that illustrates where you are currently investing your time, effort and action. Remember that there are 168 hours in every week. You need to honestly think about and account for each hour. Take enough time to think it through accurately.

SAMPLE CURRENT LIFE CHART

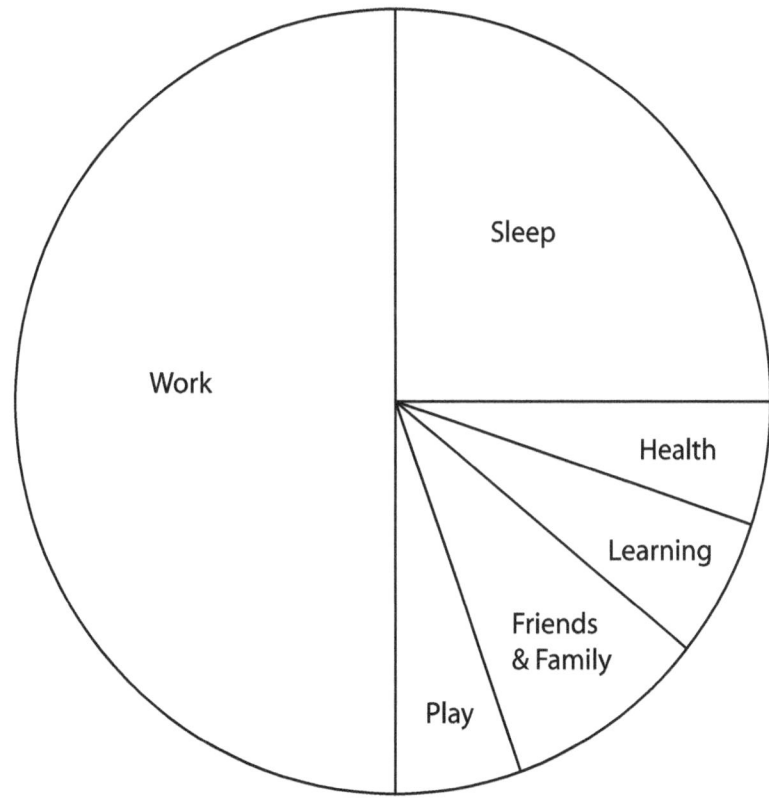

Sample Worksheet 2
How do I invest my time?

This sample schedule offers some guidelines for assigning your daily activities. We are all similar in general but amazingly different in the details. On page 18, fill in every hour of each day, including sleeping, with your current weekly activities, then step back and look at the hours you have invested in each category. Fill in *all* spaces (*see Monday below*).

SAMPLE CURRENT LIFE SCHEDULE
This is a partial calendar. Fill in your complete hours on page 18!

	Monday	Tuesday	Wednesday	Thursday	Friday	Saturday	Sunday
12 am	sleep						
1 am	sleep						
2 am	sleep						
3 am	sleep						
4 am	sleep						
5 am	sleep						
6 am	wake/tea		yoga				
7 am	shower		shower				
8 am	work		work				
9 am	work					family	
10 am	work						
11 am	work						
12 pm	break	lunch	lunch	lunch	lunch		
1 pm	work					movie	
2 pm	work						study
3 pm	work			school			
4 pm	work						
5 pm	travel					dinner	
6 pm	dinner	dinner					dinner
7 pm	gym	school	dinner	dinner	dinner		
8 pm	home			study			
9 pm	tv						
10 pm	read						
11 pm	sleep						

In your notebook, list *each* different action, then add up the total hours spent per week. For instance: Work = 40 hrs.   Travel = 5 hrs.   Lunch = 7 hrs.   . . . and so on.

Add up the total hours in each category and transfer to your pie chart.

Worksheet 1
Assess how your life is structured now

After completing page 18 you will have the data needed to fill in this pie chart. This will show you at a glance where you are currently investing your time and energy on a daily basis. Refer to the sample on page 15 to help you get started. Fill out the schedule on page 18 and use your totals to fill out this chart, accounting for all 168 hours of each week. This will give you a clear graphic image to visualize how you are investing your time and effort. Always be honest!

MY CURRENT LIFE CHART

Worksheet 2
How do I invest my time?

The information you write in will help you make the changes you desire. Fill in and account for your activity **every hour** of every day of the week of your current life, then look at the hours invested in each category. Add up the hours and transfer your totals to a category slice on your pie chart on page 17. Seeing a visual map of your time helps you to visualize the detailed calendar of your daily schedule. Make sure to fill every cell of the table. *The sample worksheet on page 16 describes how to fill out this schedule.*

MY CURRENT LIFE SCHEDULE

	Monday	Tuesday	Wednesday	Thursday	Friday	Saturday	Sunday
12 am							
1 am							
2 am							
3 am							
4 am							
5 am							
6 am							
7 am							
8 am							
9 am							
10 am							
11 am							
12 pm							
1 pm							
2 pm							
3 pm							
4 pm							
5 pm							
6 pm							
7 pm							
8 pm							
9 pm							
10 pm							
11 pm							

On a separate sheet, list each of your categories and jot down the total hours invested in each area. Then transfer the totals to your current life chart on page 17.

LESSON 2:
Digging into Today and Creating Tomorrow

In this lesson you will take what you learned about your life today and start to see what you want to change, and how to make that change become a reality.

The next worksheet helps you to focus on the areas in your life—its patterns and activities—and assists in triggering new ideas and opening up possibilities for change. You can then decide how you want to change or what you want to add to create your PEAK LIFE.

Sample Worksheet 3
Review the components of your life

ASK YOURSELF

What needs more attention, improvement?
What could be a higher priority?
Is there an interest I could add or a habit I could downplay or remove?

Use the list below to help you brainstorm areas of your life that need more attention. On the next page, make notes on specific desires related to areas that are important to you.

Categories for Change	Examples of Changes to Make — Steps to Take
Appearance	New hairstyle, fresh clothes, grooming (facial, skincare, manicure)
Friends & Family	Birthdays, special occasions, remembering to send card
Learning & Creativity	Take singing or painting lessons, learn an instrument
Fitness, Health, Sports	Start yoga, begin walking daily, improve your diet, meditate, work out
Relaxation & Play	See a movie, go to a concert, play a game with friends
Finances	Review budget, meet with an accountant, balance your bank account
Relationships & Love	Be responsible to yourself and to others for the moment
Community	Volunteer to help locals, children, aging, disabled, pets
Work	Add a skill, improve performance, change jobs
Hobby	Take hobby to next level, connect with others of similar interests
Second Job	Look for other work venues or start new business from home
Cooking & Nutrition	Explore flavor and content in the kitchen
Home improvement	Cleaner air, better organization of space, remove clutter, streamline

These are only a few typical examples. Are there other aspects of your life you would like to improve? Add them to the list. Prioritize your list by numbering the most important aspect ①, the next ②, and so on. Work on one area of your life at a time, one step at a time.

> If you find this difficult, you are not alone. Patience and persistence will pay off! Keep reading and you'll see how it works—and it will work! You can do this!

Worksheet 3
Review the components of your life

Use the following list to help you brainstorm the areas of your life that may need more attention or would add greatly to your enjoyment of life.

My Categories	*My Changes — Steps to Take*
Appearance	
Friends & Family	
Learning & Creativity	
Fitness, Health, Sports	
Relaxation & Play	
Finances	
Relationships & Love	
Community	
Work	
Hobby	
Second Job	
Cooking & Nutrition	
Home improvement	

Fill out and prioritize your personal list by numbering the most important aspect ①, the next ②, and so on. You can work on one area of your life at a time, one step at a time. Do things that directly relate to your goal. Of the 168 hours in a week, you get to choose how to invest your time!

> If your life were the clay and you the sculptor, how would you change its shape? You can control the long-range development by focusing on today's reality.

LESSON 3:
Designing your PEAK Life

Now that you have some ideas of the parts of your life that you want to change, it is time to envision your new life.

On the following page you will see an example of how to write a letter to yourself, describing things you would like to do, changes you would like to make. We all have the same amount of time (24 hours each day). Establishing your priorities, scheduling time for one thing over the other, will make all the difference in your success.

Use Worksheet 4 to chart your life the way you want it to be. Don't be surprised if it is very different from Worksheet 1 in Lesson 1.

Worksheet 5 is your roadmap to making your PEAK LIFE happen. This will most likely be very different from Worksheet 2.

Write a Letter to Yourself

PEAK Agreement Letter

In order to make a change, a personal commitment or personal agreement is essential.

Many studies have shown that the act of writing an agreement letter helps to create success. Those who write down their goals are proven to accomplish them at an astonishing rate compared to those who do not write down their goals. Measurable results are shown to occur when the idea for making a specific change is transferred onto a real, physical piece of paper, a process which removes the idea from the category of wishful thoughts and feelings and places it in the category of action.

Even though you may not believe the letter will make a big difference, just write the letter and you will see what happens in the process. I was skeptical, but then did it and realized the power of this action. So please just start the letter and then finish it. You may have emotional reactions doing this, and experience different feelings. It is ok. Just go with it. This process is hard to do for some people and easier for others. You can do it. *This is our conscious mind making an agreement with our unconscious mind.*

Take a look at your new life goals and then write a letter to yourself committing/agreeing to the desired life and preparing yourself for change.

This is my sample letter for you. The next page is for you to write your own letter.

> Dear Self,
>
> Making a commitment/agreement with you is a hard thing even to begin. I want to make a better life. I trust that I will make time for the life I desire. I will write down the areas of my life I want to change and specifics that will get me to my goals. I will put the actions into my ever-changing calendar. I will check it daily and do my best to accomplish the tasks on my calendar every moment of every day. If I go off course, I feel I will get back on course and stay on course using the PEAK mantra.
>
> In general, I want to get a buddy/friend, someone to go over my goals with, to talk and meet regularly to help keep me on track. Buddy system.
>
> I want to improve my workouts to improve my overall look. I will find new classes to make this happen.
>
> I want to correct my spending and savings to have a successful retirement.
>
> I have confidence these changes will happen and I will feel super great with my new life. One foot in front of the other, one step at a time is the way to make big changes.

Please go on to the next page and make your agreement letter.

A Letter to Myself:

Sample Worksheet 4
Map your ideal life

Start to create an improved life by focusing on your new priorities and incorporating them into your daily life.

On the next page, you will complete a new pie chart that includes the component changes from your revised list (from Worksheet 3, page 21). Here is a sample that reflects a typical week. You can make your chart represent your own typical desired week.

SAMPLE IDEAL LIFE CHART

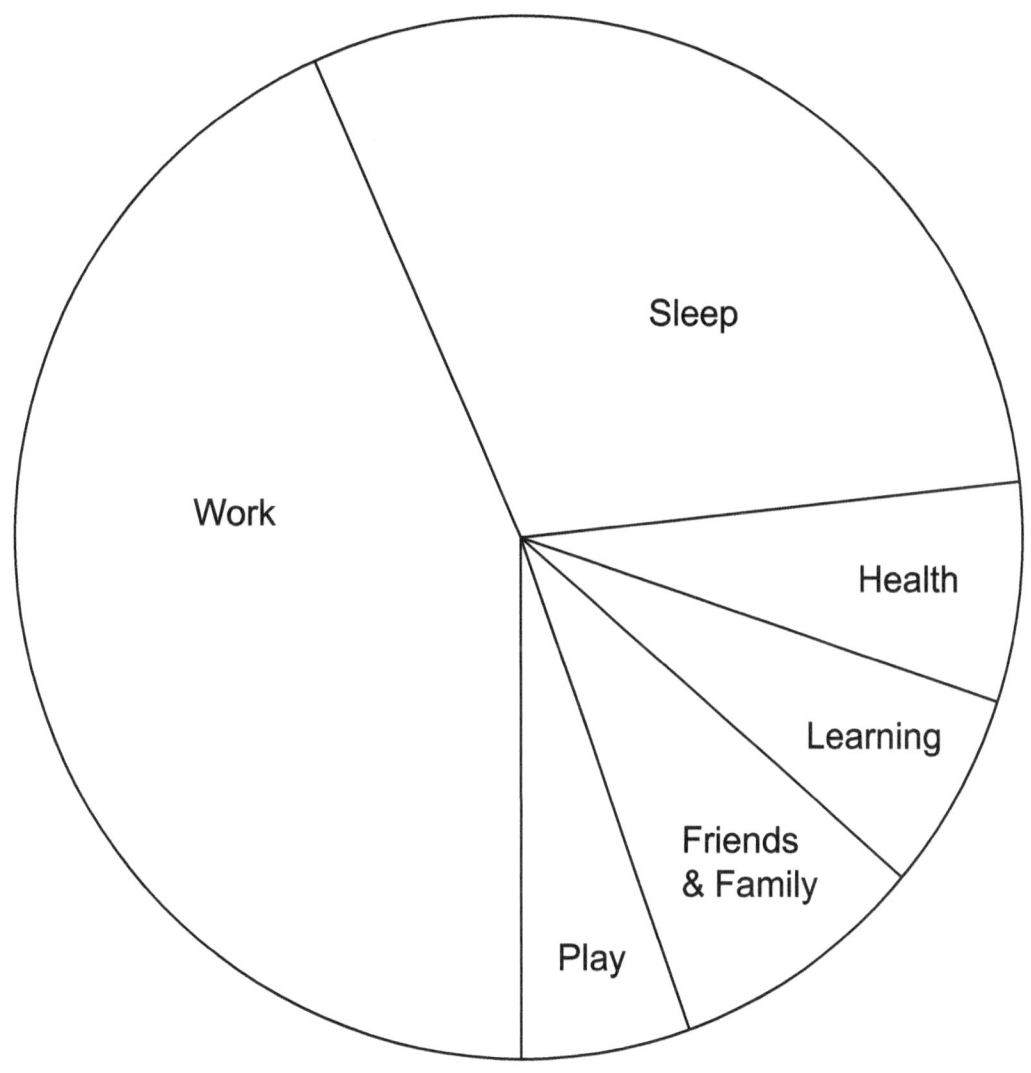

Worksheet 4
Map your ideal life

Fill out your new ideal schedule on page 27 and then complete this pie chart, including your new desired components from page 21 and your letter to yourself. You will deal with the new areas one at a time, but for now put in what you would ultimately like to see as your ideal reality.

Worksheet 5
Make time for your priorities

Tweak your schedule to include one or more new areas. Then make a new ideal life pie chart on page 26. You are doing a good job! You are making progress!

MY IDEAL or IMPROVED SCHEDULE

	Monday	Tuesday	Wednesday	Thursday	Friday	Saturday	Sunday
12 am							
1 am							
2 am							
3 am							
4 am							
5 am							
6 am							
7 am							
8 am							
9 am							
10 am							
11 am							
12 pm							
1 pm							
2 pm							
3 pm							
4 pm							
5 pm							
6 pm							
7 pm							
8 pm							
9 pm							
10 pm							
11 pm							

LESSON 4:
Making your PEAK Life a Reality

Take a look at your priorities you put on Worksheet 5. Pick one area of your new life that you would like to change or incorporate. Put it on your calendar to make the time to commit to this change. It will take time to make that change and get comfortable with it. Make sure that the change takes root and becomes a natural part of your life.

Check in with your calendar every day to see how you are doing with your new schedule. Periodically re-evaluate, envision and refine.

When you've incorporated the new area(s) smoothly into your life, review your list and choose another desired area to add. Complete a revised Worksheet 5 when you need to. Keep it going!

There is an extra set of the five worksheets at the end of the book.

Congratulations on thoughtfully completing your PEAK Method Workbook!

Time is your tool — you are the designer of your day.

PEAK Method Review

ASK YOURSELF

What area of my life am I committed to changing now?

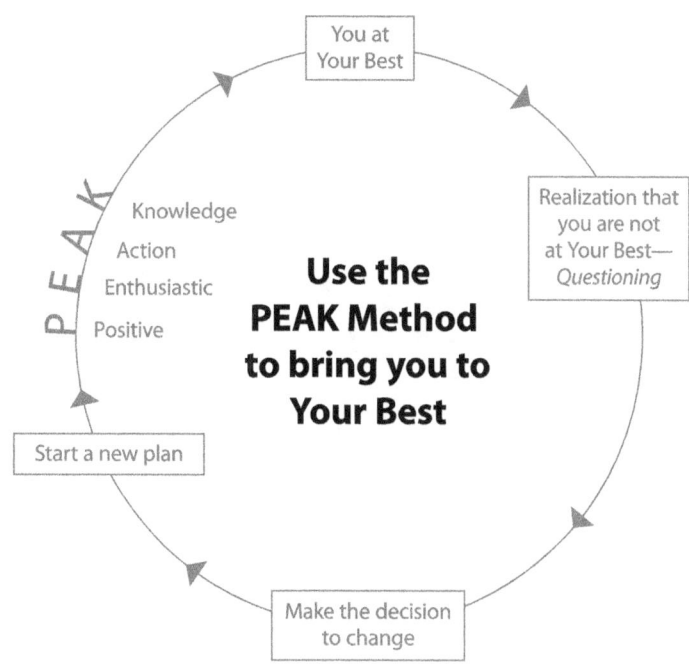

Use the **PEAK Method** cycle to change your life. Make notes in a small notebook to help you identify where you are and what steps you need to take to get where you want to be. Review your calendar and notebook daily as a way of life.

Remember: Add to your life only those steps and actions that pertain to your goal! Each time you find that you are not at your best, follow the **PEAK Method** cycle. Your personal improvement is your top priority.

IMPORTANT: Go back to the beginning of this PEAK booklet and keep learning from the **PEAK Method**. Keep practicing this and you will continually renew yourself and achieve your ideal life. Memorize what PEAK stands for (page 9) and practice the PEAK Mantra (page 11).

Your life is ever-changing, positively, with the PEAK Method.

> **Happiness depends upon ourselves.**
> *Aristotle, Greek critic, philosopher, physicist & zoologist (384 BC - 322 BC)*

You may wonder, "How do I shorten the PEAK cycle?"

There's no shortcut, but you can identify and go through the process more quickly, shortening the cycle to get to your PEAK happiness. In moments of doubt, the sooner you notice any feelings of negativity or dissatisfaction, the sooner you can employ the PEAK Method to achieve your best. It can be challenging to accept the need for change, but once you see the truth you can no longer deny that there is a better way.

This book is the real deal. If you're willing to see yourself clearly, you'll be able to use your power to change. Using the PEAK Method is your key.

The PEAK Method is changing people's lives!

As you find this method is beginning to work for you, you can also begin to do your part by helping others reach toward their own full potential, spreading enthusiasm and power from your center outward.

Please visit us at

www.peakmethod.com

About The Author

SUSAN FLEMING is a healthy living coach and nationally certified massage therapist specializing in chronic muscle pain relief and personal improvement motivation. Her coaching and massage therapy practices combine to motivate the individual to be connected physically, emotionally, mentally and spiritually with a plan of action, creating a life designed to be fulfilling on all levels.

Susan is the owner of **The Relaxation Center** in Belmont, California. In her many years of body-mind coaching she has continued to share her belief in each person's ability to transform his or her life for the better. Her teaching inspires sustainable and positive life changes.

SUSAN FLEMING
Speaker, Author and Coach

During her early career in hotel and restaurant management, Susan developed a passion for bringing out the best in her employees and helping them find the strength and power within themselves to achieve their personal and professional goals. "I made a commitment to live a healthy life. I see the significant value of my life lessons and want to share my proven strategies with others. My goal is to work toward a better world, one healthy person at a time."

Further consultation and personal guidance is available to support your personal goals. Now you can benefit from Susan's expertise and create your enjoyable life!

Susan Fleming
CMT CAMTC #9616
NATIONALLY CERTIFIED NCBTMB #2445-00
(650) 591-2303
susan@peakmethod.com

www.peakmethod.com

My Notes:

EXTRA PEAK METHOD WORKSHEETS

One set of five worksheets

Worksheet 1
Assess how your life is structured now

After completing page 18 you will have the data needed to fill in this pie chart. This will show you at a glance where you are currently investing your time and energy on a daily basis. Refer to the sample on page 15 to help you get started. Fill out the schedule on page 18 and use your totals to fill out this chart, accounting for all 168 hours of each week. This will give you a clear graphic image to visualize how you are investing your time and effort. Always be honest!

MY CURRENT LIFE CHART

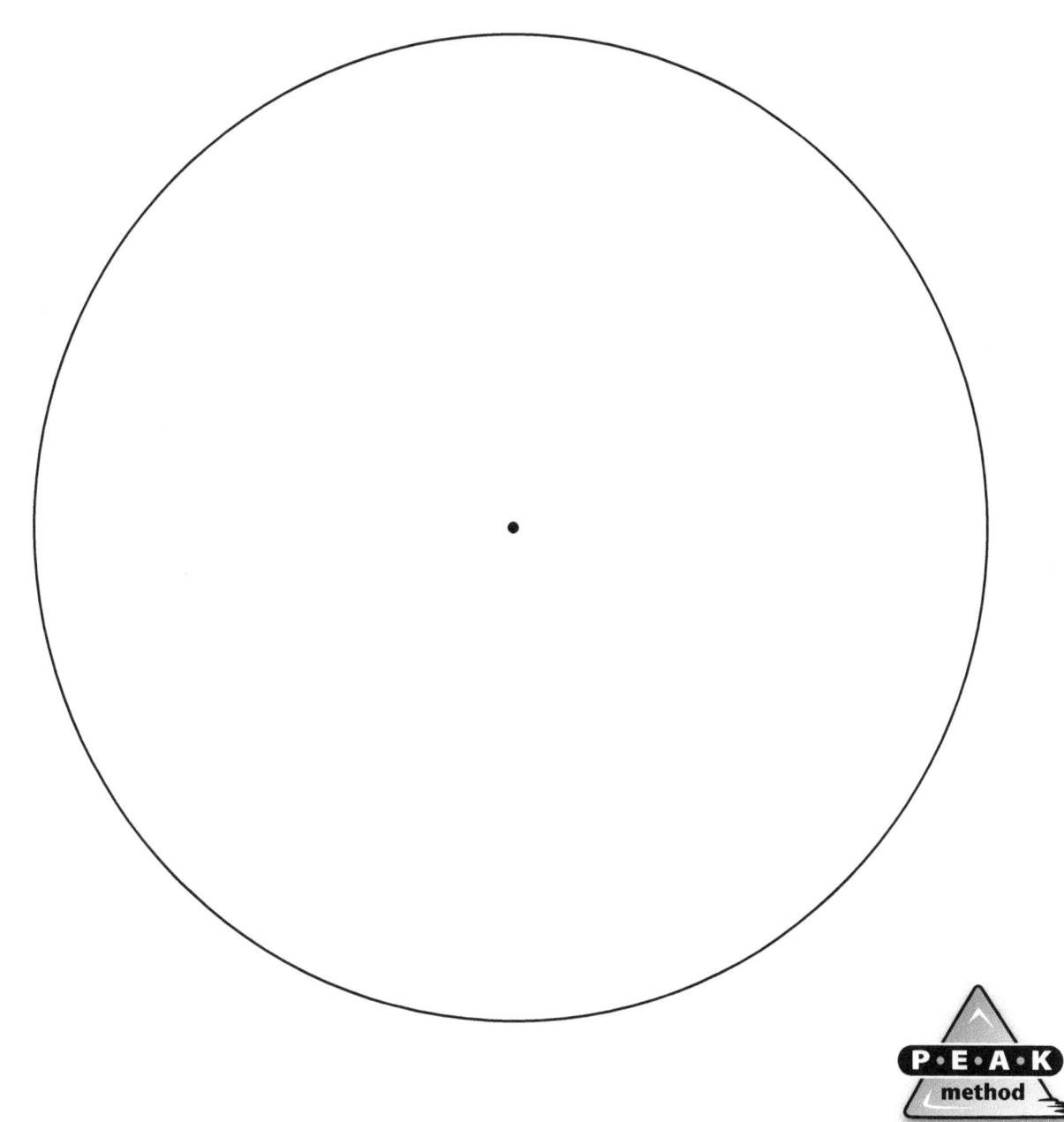

Worksheet 2

How do I invest my time?

The information you write in will help you make the changes you desire. Fill in and account for your activity **every hour** of every day of the week of your current life, then look at the hours invested in each category. Add up the hours and transfer your totals to a category slice on your pie chart on page 17. Seeing a visual map of your time helps you to visualize the detailed calendar of your daily schedule. Make sure to fill every cell of the table. *The sample worksheet on page 16 describes how to fill out this schedule.*

MY CURRENT LIFE SCHEDULE

	Monday	Tuesday	Wednesday	Thursday	Friday	Saturday	Sunday
12 am							
1 am							
2 am							
3 am							
4 am							
5 am							
6 am							
7 am							
8 am							
9 am							
10 am							
11 am							
12 pm							
1 pm							
2 pm							
3 pm							
4 pm							
5 pm							
6 pm							
7 pm							
8 pm							
9 pm							
10 pm							
11 pm							

On a separate sheet, list each of your categories and jot down the total hours invested in each area. Then transfer the totals to your current life chart on page 17.

Worksheet 3
Review the components of your life

Use the following list to help you brainstorm the areas of your life that may need more attention or would add greatly to your enjoyment of life.

My Categories	My Changes — Steps to Take
Appearance	
Friends & Family	
Learning & Creativity	
Fitness, Health, Sports	
Relaxation & Play	
Finances	
Relationships & Love	
Community	
Work	
Hobby	
Second Job	
Cooking & Nutrition	
Home improvement	

Fill out and prioritize your personal list by numbering the most important aspect ①, the next ②, and so on. You can work on one area of your life at a time, one step at a time. Do things that directly relate to your goal. Of the 168 hours in a week, you get to choose how to invest your time!

If your life were the clay and you the sculptor, how would you change its shape? You can control the long-range development by focusing on today's reality.

Worksheet 4
Map your ideal life

Fill out your new ideal schedule on page 27 and then complete this pie chart, including your new desired components from page 21. You will deal with the new areas one at a time, but for now put in what you would ultimately like to see as your ideal reality.

MY IDEAL LIFE CHART

Worksheet 5
Make time for your priorities

Tweak your schedule to include one or more new areas. Then make a new ideal life pie chart on page 26. You are doing a good job! You are making progress!

MY IDEAL or IMPROVED SCHEDULE

	Monday	Tuesday	Wednesday	Thursday	Friday	Saturday	Sunday
12 am							
1 am							
2 am							
3 am							
4 am							
5 am							
6 am							
7 am							
8 am							
9 am							
10 am							
11 am							
12 pm							
1 pm							
2 pm							
3 pm							
4 pm							
5 pm							
6 pm							
7 pm							
8 pm							
9 pm							
10 pm							
11 pm							

www.ingramcontent.com/pod-product-compliance
Lightning Source LLC
Chambersburg PA
CBHW081219230426
43666CB00015B/2796